The Greatest Showman Medley

Words and Music by Benj Pasek and Justin Paul
Arranged by Lindsey Stirling

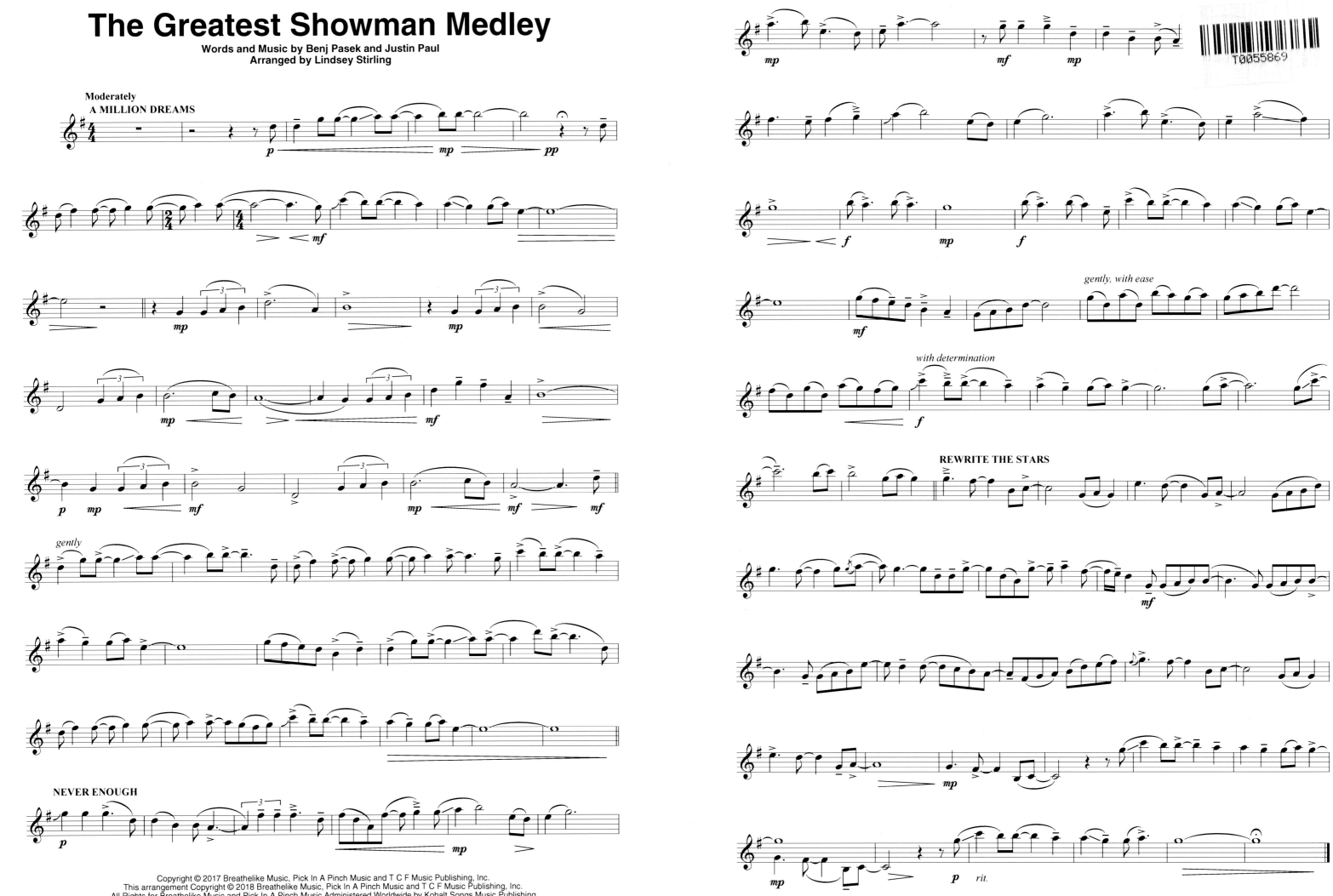

T0055869

THE GREATEST SHOWMAN
MEDLEY FOR VIOLIN

AS PERFORMED BY

Lindsey Stirling

Demonstration and backing tracks are included.
Use the unique code below to access audio tracks online for download or streaming.

MEDLEY INCLUDES:

A MILLION DREAMS

NEVER ENOUGH

RE-WRITE THE STARS

www.lindseystirling.com
www.facebook.com/lindseystirlingmusic
twitter.com/LindseyStirling

HL00276949

To access audio visit:
www.halleonard.com/mylibrary

Enter Code

7488-2862-8481-1721

EXCLUSIVELY DISTRIBUTED BY
HAL•LEONARD®
7777 W. BLUEMOUND RD. P.O. BOX 13819 MILWAUKEE, WI 53213

12-19
U.S. $9.99

VIOLIN SOLO

Audio Access
Included

THE GREATEST SHOWMAN
MEDLEY FOR VIOLIN

AS PERFORMED BY

Lindsey Stirling

WORDS AND MUSIC BY BENJ PASEK AND JUSTIN PAUL

FOX MUSIC™